813.54
H
Hobson, Linda
Understanding
Walker Percy